The Hawaiian Quilt

A Spiritual Experience

MUTUAL PUBLISHING

The Hawaiian Quilt

A Spiritual Experience

Reflection on its History, Heritage,
Designing, Quilting Methods and Patterns

By Poakalani and John Serrao

Mutual Publishing

Library of Congress Catalog Card
Number: 97-72937

Design by Mei Chi Chin

First Printing, August 1997
Second Printing, August 1998
  2 3 4 5 6 7 8 9

ISBN 1-56647-172-9

Mutual Publishing
1215 Center Street, Suite 210
Honolulu, Hawaii 96816
Telephone (808) 732-1709
Fax (808) 734-4094
e-mail: mutual@lava.net

Printed in Australia

*H*awaiian *Q*uilting,
*A L*egacy

Hawaiian Quilting is more than just an art,
It is a discipline.
The ability to create with your own heart a legacy
of everlasting beauty.
The ability to open up your mind
to a world of Heaven sent Spirituality.
Hawaiian quilting is more than just a stitch
more than just a tuck
and more than just an appliqué.
Hawaiian quilting is Love.
It is your deepest, sincerest feelings,
coming forth from your heart through your hands
on to a master piece of Hawaiian Ingenuity.
And it is yours and only yours to share for eternity.

Poakalani

$\mathcal{D}$edication

. . . .

To our Heavenly Father, creator of all that was, is and will be, guide us in our teachings, that the knowledge we pass on to others will be of benefit to all. *Me Ke Aloha Ke Akua*

To our *Kupuna*, for their legacy of the art of Hawaiian quilting which has been handed down in our families from one generation to another. It is through their love, dedication and creativity that we are able to see the beauty of the islands put down on fabric and sewn together to form the most treasured heritage of our Hawaiian people the "Hawaiian Quilt".

To the quilters of Hawai'i, our deepest appreciation for your dedication and trust in our journey to preserve the cultural heritage of Hawai'i.

To our children Joseph, Raelene, Wilhelmina and John Jr. Thank you for your knowledge, help and patience in helping to perpetuate our family legacy.

*T*able of *C*ontents

John Serrao and Poakalani

*I*ntroduction by *P*oakalani

It was in the mid-1960's when my husband and I first started on our family's legacy to perpetuate the art and traditions of the Hawaiian quilt. Up to then, our time was taken up with the trials of life and raising a family. One day as we started to clean up and discard the old collectibles in our home, we came across the two barrels of quilt patterns left to me by my grandmother, Mrs. Caroline Speckman Correa. After perusing through its contents and reflecting on times past, our feelings seemed to merge as our thoughts reflected on the quilting circles in both of our family homes. We reminised on how we watched our *kupuna* gathered around the quilts with their needles, sharing their life experiences, and remembered the delight they shared when completing a quilt.

After rummaging through the designs, I started on my first Hawaiian quilted top. I discovered that even though I had one hand, I had a special gift. I was able to quilt and also teach others. My husband John, with no experience in art or designing, was able to draw upon the feelings of our *kupuna* and create designs reflecting upon the cultural heritage of Hawai'i. It seemed as though our life together was predestined. With my quilting and his designing we are able to share out talents throughout the state, nationally and internationally.

Kapa Kuiki-History
The Royal Quilting Circle
· ·

Records and history tells us that on a beautiful Hawaiian April day in 1820 the Royal women, High Chiefess Kalakua, High Chiefess Namahana and two royal wives of High Chief Kalanimoku, attended the first sewing circle on the brig *Thaddeus*. The royal women who were already astute in the fine art of mending and sewing were given a most unique opportunity to learn patch-work sewing. It was here a form of quilting was introduced.

As time passed, patch-work sewing became one of the domestic duties taught by the missionary women to the young Hawaiian girls. The young Hawaiian girls took on this new domestic duty with great diligence and skill. Even before the missionaries came to the islands, the Hawaiians were already sewing and mending, but their needles were made of crude bone and natural materials. When the traders, whalers and then missionaries came with their scissors, needles and thread it made clothes easier to create and further enhanced the Hawaiians sewing and artistic skills.

While the Hawaiian women were learning western ways and a new skill in quilting, they were being stripped of their very livelihood. They lost theirs gods, language, religion and traditions, but saw the opportunity to preserve some part of their past onto the quilts.

What started with the sewing of small patches changed into a creative, artistic and cultural endeavor. The Hawaiian women were able to take large sheets of material, fold them into equal parts and cut out their unique designs. The extra material was then given back to the missionaries for their own quilts.

The designs which make Hawaiian quilts uniquely Hawaiian embodied the very essence of the Hawaiian people. They were able to take their culture, religion, heritage and life and place it onto a quilt where no one could ever take it away again. They were able to take their legends, the beauty that surrounded them, their family and carefully design and quilt its meaning onto fabric.

The Hawaiian quilt preserved their old ways while they learned to live in a new world. Hawaiian quilting was not just a domestic duty, it became part of their life. Every stitch had meaning and every part of the design had a purpose. Hawaiian quilting became an art form. Hawaiian quilting became the every essence of being Hawaiian.

Today, two direct descendants from those royal women in the first quilting circle are still passing on the traditions of Hawaiian Quilting— John and Poakalani Serrao. Little did they realize that when their ancestors attended the first quilting circle aboard the *Thaddeus* that 175 years later they too would be passing on those quilting traditions. What started with only four Royal women today numbers in the thousands.

What started with using only cotton sheeting material brought in by the traders, the basic colors were confined to only what was available like, red, blue, green, and yellow on a muslin background. Today, with the wide variety and vibrancy of colors and various fabrics, the Hawaiian quilt has taken on a new dimension incorporating not only the past but the present and the future in its designs and colors. In the past, the Hawaiians used only two colors for their quilts; today, the colors are much bolder, brighter and beautiful.

Quilts in American Samoa

To give someone an original Hawaiian quilt pattern was considered a sign of friendship; but, to actually give that person a completed quilt made by yourself is the greatest symbol of love.

Kapa Kuiki-Designing

There was never any doubt that missionaries taught the Hawaiian people how to quilt. However, if one was to trace the designs of the Hawaiian quilt, they would have to go back before the arrival of the explorers, traders and missionaries.

Using only what nature provided, the artistic talent and ingenuity of the Hawaiian people was evident in all aspects of their everyday life. Without the use of any metal tools they were able to produce their canoes, calabashes, idols and other items using the stone adze. Their artistry was also seen in the designs printed on the *tapa* cloth made of tree bark, sketched on the calabash, etched on their weapons, weaved into their *lauhala* mats, sewn onto their feather capes, helmets and baskets.

With the arrival of the explorers, traders and missionaries, the Hawaiian's old way of life was lost. The needs of everyday life were replaced with goods from the Western world. No longer was there any need to produce the *tapa*, carve the *koa* bowls, the canoes, gods, *lauhala* mats, cooking utensils and weapons. All of this was replaced and the artistry that went with it was set aside.

The missionary women taught the Hawaiian women how to make quilts, but the Hawaiian women saw no meaning in patchwork quilts. The patchwork quilts had no stories or traditions they could relate to. The Hawaiian women therefore gave the quilts a meaning and a purpose for themselves. They placed all of their traditional designs onto the quilt and made their own unique form of quilting—The Hawaiian Quilt.

The designs of the Hawaiian quilt are a reflection of the talents and beliefs of our ancestors or *kupuna*. The Hawaiian people were afforded through the quilt a new medium to express their talents by creating special designs. The quilt designs were patterned after the desires of their ancestors and their longing for the return of their gods; to document the beauty of the land, the heritage of their legends. The designs also took the form of flowers, foliage, trees, animals, and artificats to protest changes and to reflect their everyday life and dreams.

The designs of the Hawaiian quilt also had taken a profound step into the documentation of the Hawaiian culture. Designs were fashioned to document certain events in Hawai'i's history— a visible history of a family genealogy, a vision into the future for whom the quilt is intended— and like the European crests or coat of arms, the design on the Hawaiian quilt was a visible emblem of a Hawaiian family line.

The designs were a carefully guarded secret. In old Hawai'i every family had their own crest, and to wear someone else's crest surely meant death. So when the Hawaiian women created their quilts, each design was an original. To copy someone's design was considered stealing. If you took someone else's design, it was believed that you also took part of the spirit of the designer and quilter. When a design was stolen great shame was also brought upon the person who took the design. Every family had a designer, and if you stole someone else's design, you were considered less of an artist.

Every portion of the quilt had a meaning from the designs to the quilting lines. The Hawaiians had a reason and purpose in everything they did and quilting was no exception.

John Serrao showing Quilter June Gerber designing methods.

Never sit on a quilt. It was considered disrespectful to the designer and quilter.

Description of the Hawaiian Quilt

· ·

The Hawaiian quilt reflected the religious beliefs of old Hawai'i. The main parts of the quilt was its center which is made both solid and with an opening, the branches, the single full design and the quilting. Each of its parts had a special meaning for the designer and also the quilter.

Ulu **or Breadfruit**
Poakalani Collection
Copyright 1972

Mango
Poakalani Collection
Copyright 1972

Center

The Center of the Hawaiian Quilt

Like all indigenous beliefs, the Hawaiians believed: Hawai'i is the center of Mother Earth; Hawai'i is the gateway to the spiritual world; Hawai'i is the source of all the love and compassion in the world. This was, is and will continue to be the beliefs of our ancestors. Without a center, peace, love and hope was unattainable. When one's center was balanced, the life force and life energy was able to flow freely. The Hawaiian women believed in this knowledge, and they placed their center onto every single quilt that they made.

The center of the quilt documented the center of mother earth and the center of one's self or the quilter. One's strength lies within the love and compassion of one's center, deep set and most of all forgiving.

Quilter Tia Waxman in Poakalani's class, basting her quilt.

Ulu Elekini
Poakalani Collection
Copyright 1972

Open Center

The Quilt with an
Opening in the *Piko* or Center

The Hawaiians believed both in the physical and spiritual world and that the two worlds were as one. Speaking with family members who had already passed on was not an unfamiliar sight because they did it everyday. If you look back on the Hawaiian's beliefs, they believed that certain areas on each island had gateways between the physical and spritiual worlds, and that people could travel between the two.

Our ancestors believed that they could easily enter the spiritual world to confer with their gods and ancestors and return to the physical world unharmed. *Ho'oponopono* is based on the belief of *Nana I Ke Kumu* or look to the source. The source is not always physical and, through the spirits, the answers to a certain problem could be found.

Using this belief, the Hawaiian women created open centers on some of their quilts. The opening represented the gateway to the spiritual world. It was always interesting watching the Hawaiian women make their quilts. The women spoke to their quilt as if it was a person and it embodied a spirit. For example, during prayer a person opens their heart to a spiritual world.

When a family had a party, all the quilts were brought out and beautifully displayed on the beds. This was done so the people who made the quilts would also be remembered during the celebration.

***Panini* or Cactus**
Poakalani Collection
Copyright 1992

Solid Center

The Quilt with a Solid Center

A solid center usually depicted the core of the family, the center of one's life. It is the source, strength and the roots of the family and individual. That is why when a quilt was made, the center was always completed first because it was the quilter's center, and focus point, and they believed that is where their life and energy force came from.

Quilter Hiroka Vaughan with Poakalani displaying her quilt.

The Hawaiian quilt design was cut from a single piece of material to signify the purity of the spirit and the purity of the blood line unbroken.

***Pua Melia* - Plumeria**
Poakalani Collection
Copyright 1972

Branches

The Branches of the Quilt
the Ha-stems or Breath of Life
· ·

The Hawaiians believed in a strong spiritual and physical center, but they also believed in growth. Our center reflects our personalities and the life we live. From our centers we reach out to the world and share what has been given us. We reach out to our families and friends. Without a strong center and roots we become weak and disillutioned, and never reach out and grow. The Hawaiian designers who had this strong belief always designed with branches reaching out toward the quilt.

The branches of the quilt extending from the center and reaching out to the borders represented personal and family growth. It also represented the spiritual growth of one's soul, its love reaching out to all.

Poakalani's quilt class in American Samoa.

The Hawaiian word for quilting is KUIKI.

The *Lei* or Border

. . . .

Leis are the international symbol of Hawai'i. If you went any-where in the world and wore a *lei* people knew that you were from Hawai'i. Everyone wore *a lei*, from beautiful hand crafted feather *lei* to floral *lei*. *Lei* expressed status, beauty and especially love. *Lei* were made from feathers, beautiful flowers and greenery, and they were made with love and given with love. The Hawaiian women loved the meaning of the *lei* and also incorporated it onto the Hawaiian quilts.

The *lei* or border of the Hawaiian quilt depicted the lands outside of Hawai'i with its focus as Hawai'i as its center. It is considered the lands visited by the Hawaiian people and conquered with love. The *lei* also represented one's love being returned to its center.

The continuous enclosed border or *lei* of the quilt also represented the circle of life—never ending and continous, even after death.

Each quilt design carried a special meaning. It was made with a special purpose, reason and a person in mind. It was designed to preserve our cultural heritage, our family history, legends, environment and special loves. As such, the quilt design was cherished by its owners because of the powers and prayers in it. Its true meaning remains only with the quilter.

There are three types of borders or *lei* common to the Hawaiian quilt.

The Border *lei*

The *lei* is made as part
of the edge of your quilt

Nanialii or Silverswords Royal Beauty
Poakalani Collection
Design Copyright 1991

HUMU - *the Hawaiian word* humu *means to sew, stitch and to seam.*

The Full *lei* or Free Standing *lei*

The *lei* is separate from your center and edging.

Ti Leaf
Poakalani Collection
Design Copyright 1991

The Attached *Lei*

The *lei* is attached to your
center design.

**Lilia O ka Awawa or Lily
of the Valley**
*Poakalani Collection
Copyright 1991*

Starting Your Quilt

Now that you have a historical background on the Hawaiian quilt you are now ready to begin.

Supplies

❖ **2 scissors**–One pair of scissors to cut your material and one to cut your paper patterns.

❖ **Needles**–#7 betweens quilting needles.

❖ **Pins**–Common pins to fasten your pattern to your material.

❖ **Sewing thread**–Dual duty plus, and quilting thread of colors matching your pattern and background material. Basting thread.

❖ **Thimbles**–It is recommended that you use a thimble when quilting to prevent injuries. Leather thimble is recommended for beginners.

❖ **Quilting Hoops**–14' quilting hoop for your cushion size quilt and larger for a full size quilt.

❖ **Batting**–Same size as appliquéd piece.

Due to the tendency of cotton and wool batting to ball up during washing, the use of polyester batting has come into frequent use. The weight of the batting will determine how pronounced the ridges of your quilt will appear. If you are a beginner it is recommended that you start with a 5 ounce batting as it will be easier for you to work with. The experienced quilter should use 8 ounce batting to better enhance their work.

- ❖ **Backing material**–2 to 4 inches larger than completed appliquéd piece. Muslin, Hawaiian Print or Calico.

- ❖ **Elastic**–1 yard, 1 inch width elastic cut into three equal pieces.

- ❖ **Safety Pins**–3 Large Safety Pins.

- ❖ **Pattern/Design**–it is recommended that you create your own pattern or design. In this manner the design would be one you can truly call your own. Let your imagination do the designing for you and let your love show in your creation.

- ❖ **Material**–2 pieces fabric: 1 for pattern, 1 for backing— contrasting colors.

When using cotton material you must preshrink your material before use. Polyester/Cotton blends are also used because of its greater selection of colors.

Cushion-Two 5/8 yard of contrasting colors. Cut into a 22" square backing and batting. Completed cushion or wallhanging 22" square.

Wall Hanging-Two 60" of contrasting colors, backing and batting.

Full Size Quilt-Two 5-1/2 yards of contrasting colors, backing and batting.

Joined to give you a 90" x 90" square.

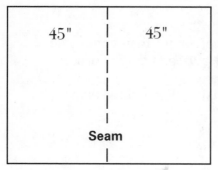

Note: 1/2 inch seam, iron open.
Fold material right side in when folding and cutting design

Queen and Kings: Two 9 yards of contrasting colors, backing and batting.

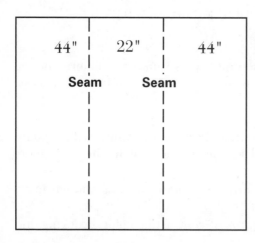

Note: 1/2 inch seam, iron open.
Fold material right side in when folding and cutting design

Never design or make a quilt with human figures. It was believed that the figures would walk at night.

$\mathcal{D}$esigning, $\mathcal{F}$olding & $\mathcal{L}$aying $\mathcal{Y}$our Quilt

The basic understanding for many people was that the quilt was always designed on a one-eighth fold or right angle. Don't limit yourself to only the one-eighth design. The (1/8) one-eight fold is the most popular fold but a (1/4) one-quarter, (1/2) one-half, and whole design gives more space and creativity. It is recommended that you cut out your design on paper so you can make any necessary changes before the final cut on material. Also, remember the width of the design. Keep the quilter in mind when designing. Keep the widths of the branches at least 1" wide. Anything smaller would make the sewing difficult. Let the design flow through the pattern. Avoid any sharp turns.

The 1/8 or right angle design

The 1/8 fold method is the most commonly used method in designing your Hawaiian quilt pattern. A design drawn in this manner will duplicate itself eight times and result in a full single piece design.

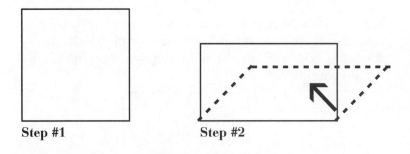

Step #1   Step #2

After completing your quilt sleep with it for one night then present it to the one you made it for. This will bind your spirit and love into the quilt.

Fold your material or paper as follows. When designing, leave at least a minimum of two inches for a cushion pattern and a minimum of four inches on the edge for a full size quilt.

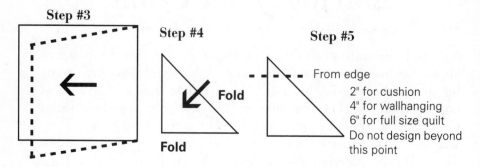

Step #3

Step #4

Fold

Fold

Step #5

From edge
2" for cushion
4" for wallhanging
6" for full size quilt
Do not design beyond
this point

Place your pattern on the folded material, pin and cut. Be sure that the edges of the pattern are located on the folded edges of your material.

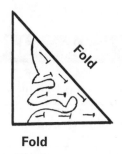

Fold

Fold

Open up your pattern and center it on your background material. Secure your pattern with common pins and baste along the edges. Remember to remove the pins after basting your design

1/4 fold design or two fold method

The 1/4 Fold or two fold method is usually used when a rectangular shaped bedspread or wall hanging is being made. The two fold method will duplicate itself four times to create your full design.

Fold your material or paper as follows. When designing, leave at least a minimum four inches on the edge for your quilt.

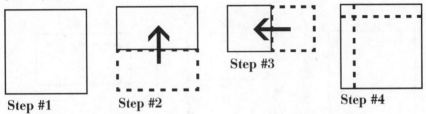

Step #1   Step #2   Step #3   Step #4

Place your pattern on the folded material, pin and cut. Be sure that the edges of the pattern are located on the folded edges of your material.

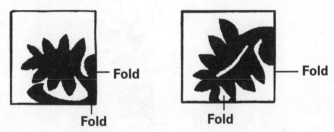

Open up your pattern and center it on your background material. Secure your pattern with common pins and baste along the edges. Remember to remove the pins after basting your design.

Tradition says that the Hawaiians only used white quilting thread to make their beautiful quilts. White quilting thread was the only color thread they had at that time.

Single Fold

The single fold method is usually used when creating a wall hanging or when a simple pattern is desired.

The single fold method will duplicate itself once and result in a full single pattern.

Fold your material or paper as follows. When designing, leave at least a minimum four inches on the edge for your quilt.

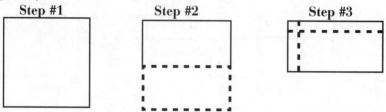

Step #1   **Step #2**   **Step #3**

Place your pattern on the folded material, pin and cut. Be sure that the edges of the pattern are located on the folded edges of your material.

Fold

Open up your pattern and center it on your background material. Secure your pattern with common pins and baste along the edges. Remember to remove the pins after basting your design.

Hawaiians dried their quilts with the design facing down. This was to protect their quilt from the sun and the design from being stolen.

No Fold

Full Pattern. Use your creativity and let it flow into your design.

When designing leave at least a minimum four inches on the edge for your quilt.

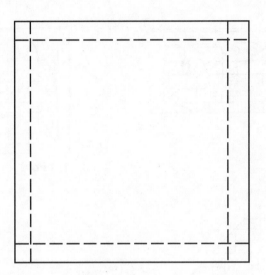

Place your pattern on the folded material, pin and cut.

Designing the *lei* or borders

When creating a *lei* for your quilt be sure that your pattern starts and ends on the folds to get a continuous design. Always design the *lei* before center design.

The **Border** *lei*. Where the *lei* is made part of the edge of your quilt.

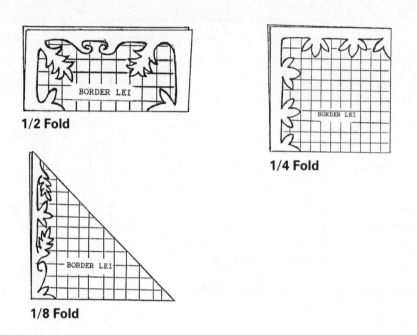

1/2 Fold

1/4 Fold

1/8 Fold

The **Attached** *lei*. Where the *lei* is attached to your center design.

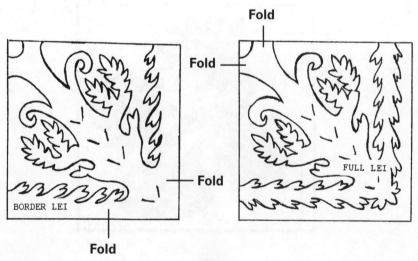

Fold

34

The Full *lei* **or Free Standing** *lei*. Where the *lei* is separate from your center design and the edge of your quilt.

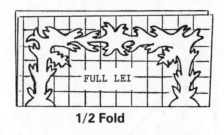

1/2 Fold

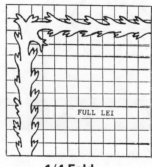

1/4 Fold

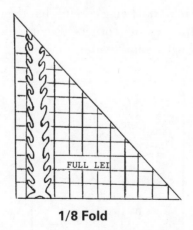

1/8 Fold

It can take from 6 months to 50 years to finish a full-size quilt depending on how much time you work on it.

Securing your pattern to the material

After your material has been folded according to the instructions, place your pattern on the material, pin it in place and cut out your pattern by following the outline of the design.

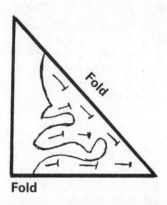

Placing your cut design on the background fabric

After your pattern has been cut, open up your pattern and center it on the background material being careful that the longer portions of the pattern are pointing to the corners. Secure your pattern to the background material with common pins.

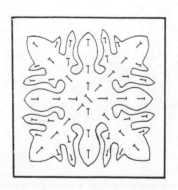

The Hawaiian word for quilt is KAPA.

Basting your pattern to the background material

Upon completing the pinning of your pattern to the background material to prevent it from shifting, you are ready to baste.

In basting, use large running stitches across the centers and approximately 1/4 inch along the entire edge of the pattern from the edge.

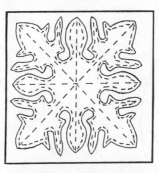

The appliqué

The appliqué stitch is simply a hemming stitch following along the edge of the pattern tucking approximately 1/8 inch under. Always tuck about an inch from where you are actually sewing

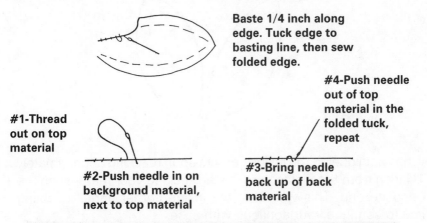

Baste 1/4 inch along edge. Tuck edge to basting line, then sew folded edge.

#1-Thread out on top material

#2-Push needle in on background material, next to top material

#3-Bring needle back up of back material

#4-Push needle out of top material in the folded tuck, repeat

Different varieties of flowers or foliage on one design was unacceptable because God and nature never intended two different species to grow out of the same root.

In order to keep your points during the appliqué, simply stay one stitch away from the point, tuck the point under your last stitch and continue your appliqué on the opposite side of the point.

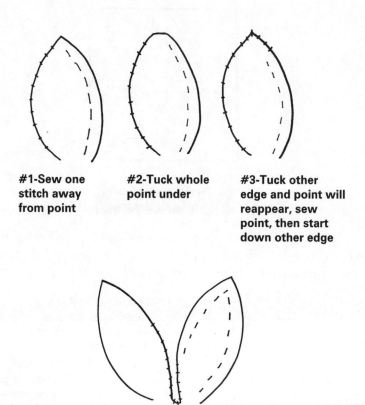

#1-Sew one stitch away from point

#2-Tuck whole point under

#3-Tuck other edge and point will reappear, sew point, then start down other edge

When appliquéing the inside corners upon reaching approximately 1/4 inch from the inside corner, start tucking your material on the opposite end. This will force the inside corner under, enabling you to continue your appliqué with ease.

KIHEI PILI - *the Hawaiian word for an appliquéd beadspread that is not quilted.*

After completing your appliqué, the next step is to combine your appliquéd piece with the batting and a backing piece of the same size.

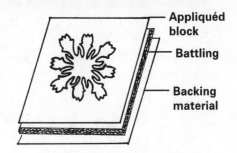

Appliquéd block

Battling

Backing material

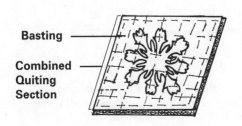

Basting

Combined Quiting Section

Upon combining all of the sections together, baste around the entire piece approximately one inch from the edges and six inches apart in the interior portion if working on a full size quilt. The basting is to prevent your batting and back piece from shifting.

The last step to take before quilting is to set up your quilting section on a stretcher frame or a hoop. The quilting hoop is preferred due to its portability and it is easy to transport. Set up your hoop in the center of your quilting section and remember that it is preferable to start from the center and work outward.

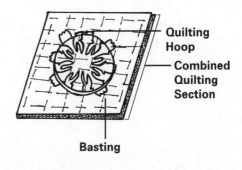

Quilting Hoop

Combined Quilting Section

Basting

Never use a pattern belonging to someone else. The spirit of the design is not yours and could sometimes bring bad luck.

Quilting

Your quilting stitch can be described as a very small running stitch or an up and down stitch. A quilter is judged by the number of stitches per inch. More stitches per inch indicates the expertise of the quilter. Ten to twelve stitches per inch is the usual indicator of an expert quilter. Though smaller stitches are recommended, the consistency of the stitches is most important.

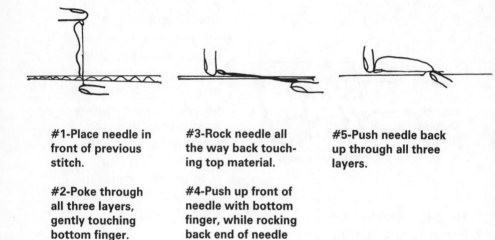

#1-Place needle in front of previous stitch.

#2-Poke through all three layers, gently touching bottom finger.

#3-Rock needle all the way back touching top material.

#4-Push up front of needle with bottom finger, while rocking back end of needle to top material.

#5-Push needle back up through all three layers.

Echo Quilting - This type of quilting followed the outline of the pattern and flowed to the edge of the quilt borders.

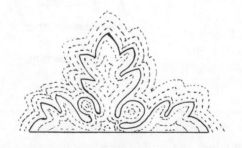

Definitive Quilting- This is used when the quilter wants to define the pattern being quilted and to represent the flower or leaf in its closed likeness.

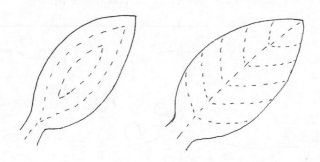

When working on your middle, quilt towards the center or work inward towards each other. When working the background, quilt towards the outside edges.

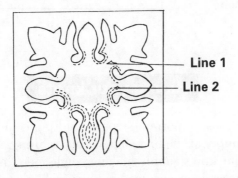

When you begin your Hawaiian quilt use a #7 quilting needle for basting, appliqué and quilting instead of three different needles for each process. Your fingers will get comfortable with the needle through the basting and appliqué stage so when you start quilting, you will be comfortable with the needle and quilting will be much easier.

Hawaiian quilting is done by following the outline of the pattern. Use your fingers as a guide to measure the spacing between each line. Most quilters use their index fingers as their spacing guide. Your echo quilting stitches should be no smaller than the width of your baby finger, and no bigger than the width of you index finger.

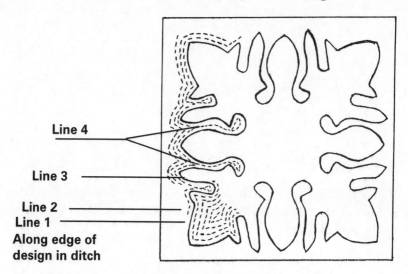

Line 4

Line 3

Line 2
Line 1
Along edge of
design in ditch

Hiding your knots

One of the most important steps in quilting is hiding your knots. This is done simply at the first step of your quilting.

To hide your knots simply make a single loop knot at the end of your thread. Insert your needle about one inch away from your starting point into the appliqued material, through the batting layer of your quilt and back out to the starting point. Pull your thread with the knot gently into the material and let it snag into the batting. At this point your knot will be locked in the batting and not visible on either side of your quilt.

Using your Hoop:

To assist you in quilting the sides and corners it is recommended that you use strips of elastic and safety pins to hold your quilt when working along the edges and corners.

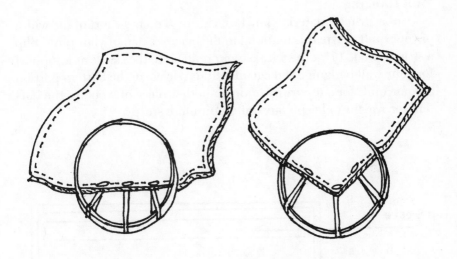

Finishing and displaying your quilt

After your quilt is done, complete your project by adding bias tape along the edges. There are several ways you can use your quilted square. The first is done by cutting a matching back piece for the quilted square. Place the additional piece of material and the quilted pieces together with the pattern facing the backing. Sew along the edges except for approximately 8 inches along one edge. Turn your quilted section right side out, fill the center with polyester filling and sew the edges. You could go a little further by adding a zipper or velcro tape.

Having your quilted square framed or making a wall hanging would be a welcome addition to any home decor. Follow the outline to make your wall hanging.

Wall Hanging

Cut a strip of material 3 inches wide by 3 inches short of the width of your quilt. Baste this material to the back portion of your quilt. Slip a strip of wood (1" x the with of your quilt) into the sleeve as a support for your wall hanging. You can also add a sleeve to the bottom portion of your quilt for support by adding another piece of wood to the bottom for weight to keep your quilt a bit more sturdy.

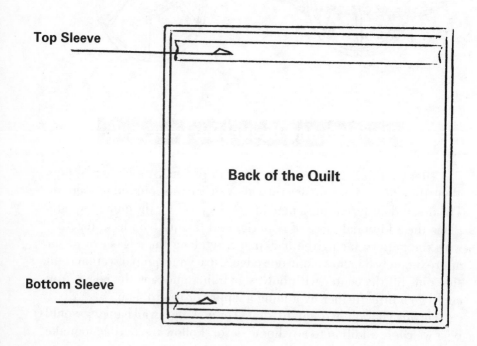

Top Sleeve

Back of the Quilt

Bottom Sleeve

Reflections
· · · · · · · · · · · · · ·

Every quilt has an inner meaning. A meaning that is known only to the designer and the quilter. That is why it was very disrespectful to change any portion of a quilt design to fit your own needs. Each design was special and for someone special and no one else.

Back in 1972 when we first came out with our quilt patterns a very generic meaning was given. Today we would like to share with you some of the meanings that inspired the making of those designs.

Quilting is like a pregnant woman. For months a woman will prepare a quilt. Her back will ache, her fingers will cramp. She will continue to suffer yet perservere for the finished result. Her eyes will tire as she quilts into the wee hours of the night. She will continue to quilt although it seems like her quilting can go on forever. Then the day comes when she places her last stitch to complete the quilt. Like the woman who just gave birth, she has forgotten the many hours of hard work and labor. The aches and pains all forgotten. All she sees in front of her is a masterpiece of beauty and love, her baby, an extended form of herself to share with the world for generations to come to carry on her memory. And yet with all she went through she's willing to get another pattern and start again.

Kanani O Ka Home
Poakalani Collection
Copyright 1972

Kanani O Ka Home - The Beauty of Home

A women was saddened by the news that her newlywed daughter was leaving the islands to live with her husband's family on the mainland. The thought of her only child living so far away in a place so foreign from the ways of the Hawaiians was very troubling to a mother who was always so protective.

One evening both mother and daughter sat on the front *lanai* of their family home spending the evening enjoying each others company. It was during this time of sharing that the young girl expressed how much she was going to miss home—the flowers that grew abundantly on the property, the sweet fragrance in the early morning air, as well as the roosters that ran throughout the property. As the young girl spoke the woman looked at her daughter leaning against the railing of the *lanai*, hoping to remember this precious moment forever. Mother and daughter spoke till early morning.

As the mother was preparing to sleep she envisioned the design of *Kanani O Ka Home*, from the plants in the yard to the roosters running around to the decorative aspect of the *lanai* railing. Each was found in the vision of this quilt pattern soon to be quilted and given to her daughter.

When the quilt was completed the mother took her quilt, wrapped herself in it and spent the evening recalling the loving memories that only a mother and daughter could have.

When it was time for the daughter to leave for the mainland, the mother presented the quilt to her daughter and told her, "Whenever you are feeling lonely or homesick, before retiring for the night, open the quilt and wrap yourself in it for the night. In doing so you will be back home with me." Through this quilt you will always remember the beauty of home—*Kanani O Ka Home*.

Plumeria
Poakalani Collection
Copyright 1972

Pua Melia-Plumeria

A mother watched as her daughter picked her plumeria flowers from the cemetery next door. A daily ritual so her daughter could entertain down at the harbor for the many tourists visiting the islands. That particular tree always gave enough flowers for her beautiful *lei*.

Returning home one day from picking her flowers, the mother asked her daughter how she was able to pick so many. Her daughter replied, " My friends help me and they tell me what branches to stand on, and the flowers I cannot reach, they gather them for me."

One morning upon waking she came across her daughter crying and found out that her favorite plumeria tree had been cut down by the maintenance workers at the cemetery.

Her mother consoled her and said that she could always find another plumeria tree. The daughter replied that it wouldn't be the same because the tree was special for her and her friends. In trying to console her daughter she decided to make her a quilt with the plumeria tree design. When the quilt was completed she presented it to her daughter. Her daugher smiled, hugging the quilt, and told her mother that she was going to show it to her friends. Walking over to the cemetery she sat where the old plumeria tree once was stood, opened up the quilt and speaking lovingly said, "Look our plumeria tree is still here and this time no one will ever cut it down."

While the mother watched her daughter, the fragrance of the plumeria blossoms filled the home. What the young girl said made this particular pattern *Kapu* or restricted. It is all right to have the same designs but wrong to alter or change any of its orginality.

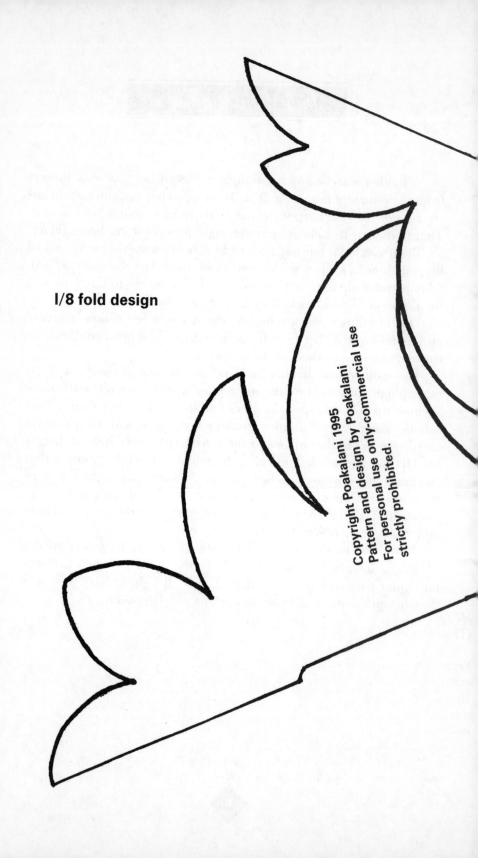

l/8 fold design

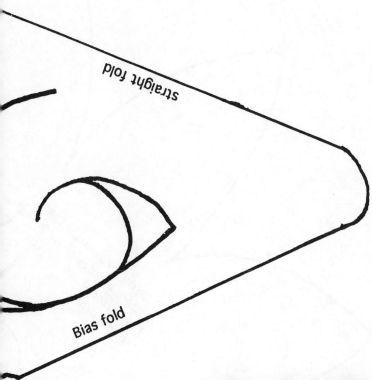

Straight fold

Bias fold

HANA O HAWAI'I
(The Birth of Hawai'i)

From out of its spiritual center comes forth the Nation of Hawai'i returning to fulfill its destiny as one of the world's leaders.

1/8 fold design

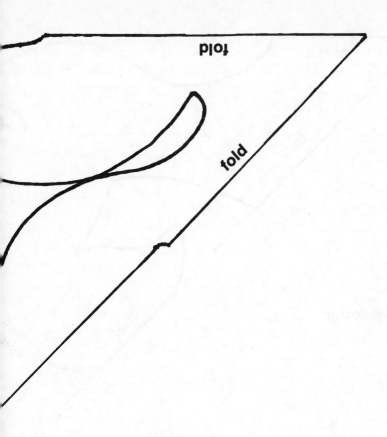

fold

fold

NAUPAKA

The legends of Hawai'i come alive in the *Naupaka* blossom. Two young lovers forbidden to see one another by their family shed their tears and produced the split flowers of the *Naupaka*. Never to meet again, the flowers grow on the beach fronts and in the mountains yearning to be reunited.

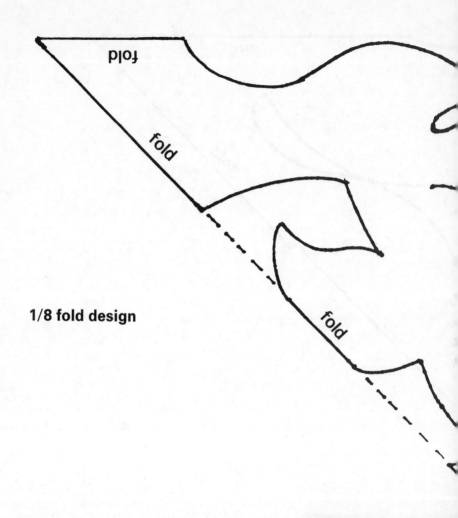

fold

fold

fold

1/8 fold design

HONU
(Sea Turtle)

Once abundant in numbers, the turtle has
been hunted to the point of near extinc-
tion. Protected as an endangered species
the turtle was once an important food
source for the Hawaiian people.

1/8 fold design

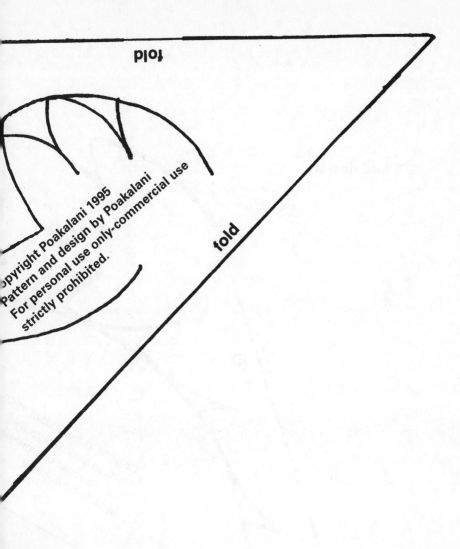

fold

fold

KAHILI O PEAHI

Kahili: The feather standard symbolic of Hawaiian Royalty. *Peahi*: The Hawaiian word for Fan. Both had their part in the History of Hawai'i and its Heritage.

1/8 fold design

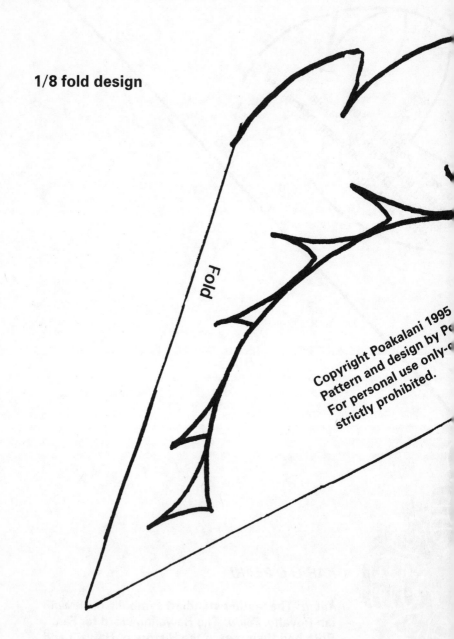

Fold

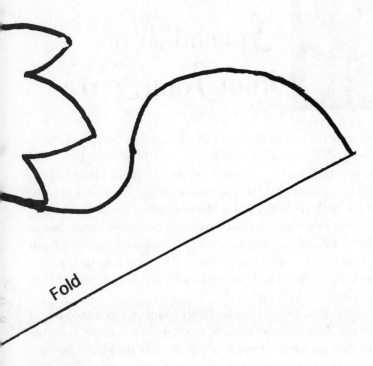

IPU
(Calabash)

Besides being used as a receptable
for their daily chores and eating
utensils, the calabash was also used
as a hula intrument to keep beat
with the rhythm of the motions.

Fold

Special Note from John Serrao

Recording and documenting one's life history is very important, and what a beautiful way to express it but on a Hawaiian Quilt. My greatest joy is seeing one of my designs develop from an idea or inspiration unto a paper pattern and then into a beautiful quilt. It is breathtaking to see the quilt designs forever documenting the life and times of the quilter. It gives me a feeling of accomplishment to know that as a cultural artist I am helping to pass on the legacy and history of our families and Hawai'i. I would like to share with you a quilt that has especially touched my life. The Damien Beatification quilt will always have a special place in my heart.

It was in 1994 that we were invited to be part of a group to travel to Belgium for the Beatification of Father Damien DeVeuster. Our role was to demonstrate the art of Hawaiian quilting. We decided that since this was a special occasion we would design a new quilt in honor of Father Damien.

The design for the quilt came in a dream. As I recall I was standing on the cliffs above Kalaupapa looking over the beauty of the land. I then saw a young priest standing nearby viewing the beautiful sight. He then turned and walked into a brush and returned carrying a shield bearing the design of the quilt. As he turned to walk down the trail to Kalaupapa there appeared to be an aura of light surrounding him as he disappeared from sight.

Upon awakening, my wife and I quickly laid out the material and cut out the design for the quilt. The quilt design was exactly the one I saw in the dream except the insignia of the Sacred Hearts was missing from the quilt. We were at a loss on how to place the Sacred Hearts insignia of Father Damien's order on the quilt. While we pondered on this problem one of our quilters, Mrs. Kay Johnson, came to class with a photo of the Sacred Heart taken from a picture window of the church that Father Damien attended in Belgium. She graciously allowed us the use of the photo to make a copy for the quilt. This copy was placed in the center of the quilt.

As we continued working on the quilt, Damien High School contacted us requesting the use of the quilt for the Damien Memorial Ceremony. To our surprise they had named the quilt the Damien Beatification Quilt.

We attended the ceremonies and at the end we were asked what our intentions were for the quilt after the Belgium ceremony. We informed the staff that we were not sure whether to donate it to the church in Kalaupapa or the church in Belgium. Soon after, Father Arsene who was standing nearby, introduced himself as the Pastor for Kalaupapa and stated that he had the perfect spot for the quilt. Right at that moment we promised that the quilt would be given to the church at Kalaupapa.

We had completed the quilt in 2 weeks and had it on display at Blessed Sacrament church in Pauoa, St. Johns Mililani, American Samoa and Chicago where it was blessed by the congregation.

We took the quilt to a Hawaiian Minister for a special blessing to reinforce the love of all Hawai'i people in the quilt. As she opened the quilt she smiled and asked where the design came from. I informed her of my dream and she started to explain the quilt.

#1. The 10 taro leaves at the bottom of the quilt signified the 10 commandments.

#2. The scallop edges on the side of the designs signified the beatitudes.

#3. The three *kukui* nut leaves on each side of the top design indicated the father, son and Holy Spirit.

The quilt explained Father Damien's role as he entered Kalaupapa. The *Kukui* leaf design indicated that Father Damien was to restore the light to Kalaupapa, as the nut from the *Kukui* tree provided light for the people of old Hawai'i. The *taro* plant on the bottom of the design indicated the family of Kalaupapa. Father Damien would gather the people together as one. The cross quilted in the center showed the plight of the sick in Kalaupapa and his role in carrying them to a dignified life. After all of this we heard the news that Pope John Paul was injured and the ceremonies were canceled for a year.

In 1995 we were unable to attend the rescheduled ceremonies due to personal reasons and felt sad over the situation until we got a phone call from Father Arsene who had asked for us at the airport thinking that we were leaving with the others. We explained our situation and he asked to use the quilt for a special mass at Kalaupapa to coincide with the beatification ceremonies in Belgium.

We happily gave the quilt to him to be forever a part of Kalaupapa and at last our mission with Father Damien came to an end.

KA PALE O KAMIANO
(The Shield of Damien)
The Damien Beatification Quilt:
Design by: Poakalani (John and Althea K. Serrao)
Quilted by: Poakalani with love stitches and touches of Haumana O Poakalani and members of the Catholic Church:
Date of Completion: April 1994

Glossary

★ **Appliquéing**- The process of sewing the top material design to the bottom material.

★ **Batting**- Polyester, wool or cotton filling used in the middle layer of a quilt.

★ **Canoes**- Ocean going vessel used by the Hawaiians to travel short and great distances.

★ **Definitive quilting**- Quilting lines defining the pattern to represent the design to its closest likeness.

★ **Echo quilting**- Quilting lines following the design of the pattern

★ **Ha**- Breath.

★ **Hanau**- Birth.

★ **Honu**- Turtle.

★ **Ipu**- Hawaiian Gourd used for storing water, food, and personal belongings . Also used as a Hawaiian Lantern.

★ **Kahili**- Feather Standard symbolic of Hawaiian Royalty.

★ **Kahili O Enia**- Pride of India. Legend has it that the Hawaiians originated from India. The demi-god Kamapua'a who was said to have come from India brought with him the Kahilis; the royal standards and *lei*.

★ **Kalaupapa**- Hansen disease settlement on the island of Moloka'i.

★ **Kanani O Amelika**- The Beauty of America.

★ **Kanani O Ka Home**- The Beauty of Home.

★ **Kapa**-Quilt.

★ **Kapu**- Sacred, restricted, to prohibit.

★ **Kihei Pili**- Appliqués bedspread that is not quilted

★ **Koa**- A large native tree. Its hard wood is used for many purposes besides canoes, bowls, and surfboards

★ **Kuiki**- Quilting, to quilt.

★ **Kukui**- Candlenut tree used for many purposes—medicinal, dying of fabric—the oil and nut was used as lighting in the Hawaiian homes.

★ **Kupuna**- Elders of the families, grandparents, ancestors.

★ **Lauhala mats**- Floor mats used by the Hawaiians made from the Pandanus leaf.

★ **Leis**- The outside decorative borders of a Hawaiian Quilt.

★ **Lilia O Ka Awawa**- Lily of the Valley.

★ **Mango**- Fruit tree.

★ **Nanialii**- Royal Beauty.

* **Naupaka**- A plant with a half blossom. Found only at the seashore and in the mountains.
* **Panini**- Cactus.
* **Peahi**- Fan.
* **Piko**- Center.
* **Plumeria**- Also known as Frangipani, scented blossom found in many varieties of colors.
* **Quilting**- The process of sewing the top appliqué pieces, the batting in the middle and the bottom material together.
* **Silversword**- Endangered plant found only on the high slopes of Haleakala, Maui.
* **Tapa**- Type of material used by the Hawaiians for clothing and bed clothes before foreign contact. Made from the bark of the *wauke* and *mamaki*.
* **Taro**- A staple eaten by the Hawaiians, also a symbol signifying family.
* **Ti Leaf**- A plant used for many purposes by the Hawaiian people. Some purposes were for food wrappers, hula skirts, for *lei* and was said to protect the people from any evil entities.
* **Ulu**- Breadfruit. A staple eaten by the Hawaiian people.

. . . .

For more information:
POAKALANI
1720 Huna Street #106
Honolulu, HI 96817